Craven – Pamlico – Carteret
Regional Library

Seeing Seabirds

By Allan Fowler

Consultants

Linda Cornwell, Learning Resource Consultant,
Indiana Department of Education

Jan Jenner, Ph.D.

Children's Press®
A Division of Grolier Publishing
New York   London   Hong Kong   Sydney
Danbury, Connecticut

Visit Children's Press® on the Internet at:
http://publishing.grolier.com

Designer: Herman Adler Design Group
Photo Researcher: Caroline Anderson

Library of Congress Cataloging-in-Publication Data

Fowler, Allan.
    Seeing seabirds / by Allan Fowler.
       p. cm. – (Rookie read-about science)
    Includes index.
    Summary: Briefly describes the appearance and habitats of birds that live and
feed near the ocean, such as the auk, puffin, pelican, gannet, cormorant, albatross,
tern, and gull.
    ISBN 0-516-21210-9 (lib. bdg.)   0-516-26568-7 (pbk.)
    1. Seabirds—Juvenile literature. [1. Seabirds. 2. Birds.] I. Titles. II. Series.
QL676.2.F686   1999   98-26398
598.177—dc21   CIP
                                       AC

The seashore is a great
place to see birds—
especially seabirds.

Seabirds usually nest on
land close to the ocean
and eat fish.

There are many different kinds of seabirds. Most are at home in the water and in the air.

You won't see a more graceful seabird than the albatross. With the help of its long wings, it can soar high over the ocean.

Albatrosses usually nest
in groups on an island.

You've probably heard
of the pelican.

Even though it's a big bird,
it has no trouble flying.

A pelican catches fish in shallow coastal waters and stores them in a big pouch hanging from its lower beak.

Young pelicans sometimes
eat fish out of their
parent's pouch.

Pelicans often nest, fly,
and fish in large flocks.

Gannets are closely related
to pelicans . . .

. . . so it's no surprise that
they live in colonies, too.

Gannets can dive from as
high as 100 feet (31 m) in
the air to catch a fish.

Blue–footed boobies

Some kinds of gannets
are called boobies.

The name booby means "foolish" or "stupid."

Sailors gave these birds that name because boobies used to land on ships and let the sailors catch them.

The sailors thought the birds were stupid because they didn't fly away.

There are several different types of boobies.

Brown boobies

Masked boobies

Another member of
the pelican family is
the cormorant.

In Asia, some people train
cormorants to help them
catch fish.

They place a special ring around the bird's neck, so it cannot swallow fish.

When the cormorant spots a fish, the bird dives down and catches it.

The people can then take the fish out of the cormorant's beak.

Auks are good swimmers,
but they have trouble
flying and walking.

Puffins are closely related
to auks. They have a
brightly colored beak.

The osprey, or fish hawk,
catches fish with the sharp
claws on its feet.

Many kinds of terns
live along the coasts
of North America.

Like many other seabirds, terns often nest in huge colonies.

Gulls—one of the most
familiar seabirds—are
closely related to terns.

Gulls often land on beaches
and beg sunbathers for food.

Even though they are often called seagulls, not all gulls live near the ocean.

They are also common along the shores of lakes and rivers—as long as the fishing is good.

Words You Know

Albatross

Auk

Booby

Cormorant

30

Gannet

Gull

Osprey

Pelican

Puffin

Tern

31

Index

About the Author

Allan Fowler is a freelance writer with a background in advertising. Born in New York, he lives in Chicago now and enjoys traveling.

Photo Credits

Photographs ©: Dembinsky Photo Assoc.: 25, 31 bottom right (Dominique Braud), 14 (J. Hawkins), 19, 30 bottom right (Stan Osolinski), 24, 31 center left (Fritz Polking); ENP Images: cover, 6, 18 top, 30 top left (Gerry Ellis); Photo Researchers: 8, 31 center right (John W. Bova), 11 (Harry Engels/National Audubon Society), 3 (Jeff Greenberg), 9 (M. J. Griffith/National Audubon Society), 12 (M. P. Kahl), 27, 31 top right (Ted Kerasote), 26 (Sven-Olof Lindblad), 18 bottom (D. Puleston); Tony Stone Images: 20 (Yann Layma), 4 (Charles Sleicher), 23, 31 bottom left (John Warden), 13, 31 top left; Visuals Unlimited: 7 (John Gerlach), 15, 16, 30 bottom left (Barbara Gerlach), 10 (Mack Henley), 28 (Dick Keen), 22, 30 top right (Joe McDonald), 5 (Rob & Ann Simpson).